Mourning, After Suicide

Lois A. Bloom

Blessed are they that mourn:
for they shall be comforted.
—Matthew 5:4, KJV

The Pilgrim Press
Cleveland, Ohio

The Pilgrim Press
Cleveland, Ohio 44115

The scripture quotation marked KJV is from the King James Version of the Bible. Excerpts marked RSV are from the Revised Standard Version of the Bible, © 1946, 1952, and © 1971, 1973 by the Division of Christian Education, National Council of Churches, and are used by permission. The biblical quotation marked NEB is from the New English Bible, © The Delegates of the Oxford University Press and the Syndics of the Cambridge University Press, 1961, 1970, and is used by permission. The biblical quotation marked TB is from page 1160 of *The Book*, Wheaton, IL: Tyndale House, 1971.

Printed in the United States of America

The paper used in this publication is acid free and meets the minimum requirements of the American National Standard for Information Sciences-Permanence of Paper for Printed Library Materials, ANSI Z39.48-1984

96 95 94 93 92   8 7 6 5 4

ISBN 0-8298-0588-5

Preface

I remember waiting that Monday night, more than three years ago, for our son, Sammy, to come home. Where was he? He was late; we had dinner waiting. His depression had returned the month before, but his father and I were optimistic that it was lifting. We had had a great weekend together.

When the doorbell rang that night, my heart skipped a beat. "Mr. Bloom," a policeman said, "do you have a son by the name of Samuel? Does he drive a white Pinto?" "Yes," my husband answered. The policeman continued, "May I come in please?" As he came into the room, I had a strange premonition. "Mr. and Mrs. Bloom, . . ." he hesitated, "you'd better sit down. I have bad news for you."

He told us our son was dead! He had driven off a cliff near the ocean's edge earlier that evening. A suicide.

Searching for comfort, I found myself reaching back in time to those years when my mother rocked me to sleep in her arms. I began to rock. "O my God!" I screamed. Tears streaked my face. The nightmare began.

In the weeks and months that followed, the questions came. "Why did this happen?" "What was so terrible in our son's life that he felt the need to end his life?" "Why would a tragedy like this happen to people like us?"

We had a good marriage and family life. Our lives revolved around our three children and the church. We communicated well with the children. They were great kids and didn't have problems with drugs or alcohol. My husband and I were both active in scouting and the PTA. We taught church school, worked with youth groups, served on church boards. As a family, we attended church regularly. Our son was good-looking, bright, ambitious, well liked. He had a love of life and a special way with people. Until he was 22, he never had a serious problem in his life. His depression appeared after having several stressful experiences when he was a college junior.

And the questions continued: "Where was God?" "Why hadn't God intervened?" "Has God forgiven and accepted our son?"

In this booklet I will share thoughts on some of these questions, the grieving process, and some feelings and emotions. The term survivor here describes one who is a remaining family member, a loved one, or a significant other of someone who has completed suicide. I am a survivor.

For the past two years, my husband and I have been co-leaders of the Suicide Support Group of the Los Angeles Suicide Prevention Center, a program for family members who have lost someone through suicide. During this time, I have listened and shared with many survivors. There is a common bond among survivors, regardless of whether they've lost a parent, spouse, brother, sister, child, boyfriend, or girlfriend.

Gratefully, during my grief, I have had support from a loving network of family, friends, church family, counselors, and a support group. During those first weeks, and months, I was devastated and felt so alone and different. I wondered, "Could anyone ever understand how I felt?" If you have those feelings, I know how it feels. May this booklet contribute to your finding your way through that bleak time to a better tomorrow.

Surviving—A Heavy Load

I have relived the weeks before our son's suicide over and over again, wondering whether I could have prevented his death. Most of the survivors I've talked with have expressed similar feelings. One mother, who had a terrible fight with her daughter before her suicide, said, "All of her friends knew. She had talked to them about killing herself. They didn't believe her. None of them told me. I had no idea." A sister told me, "I never realized my sister was so desperate. She was so good at covering up her real feelings."

Dr. Edwin Shneidman, professor of thanatology at UCLA, co-founder of the Los Angeles Suicide Prevention Center, and author of numerous books on suicide, writes in the Foreword to *Survivors of Suicide:* "I believe that the person who commits suicide puts his psychological skeleton in the survivor's emotional closet—he sentences the survivor to deal with many negative feelings and, more, to become obsessed with thoughts regarding his own actual or possible role in having precipitated the suicidal act or having failed to abort it."

Suicide casts a heavy burden on the survivors. Failing to keep a loved one alive, or even to be aware of the signs of suicide, hurts deeply.

And [David] the king was deeply moved, and went up to the chamber over the gate, and wept; and as he went, he said, "O my son Absalom, my son, my son Absalom! Would I had died instead of you."

—2 Samuel 18:33, RSV

Grief Work

As a survivor, you are now faced with dealing with the issues of grief. This is often referred to as Grief Work. Erich Lindemann, in his book *Beyond Grief*, discusses this time: "Grief work has to do with the effort of reliving and working through in small quantities events which involved the now-deceased person and the survivor. . . . Each item of this shared role has to be thought through, *pained* through."

Confronting each of the remembered shared experiences that you had with the deceased is extremely difficult. It takes a great deal of time and energy to face each of the issues. I found this to be painful and wondered if it was necessary. Looking back on that time period, I now realize how important it was to deal head-on with whatever was distressing me. Some survivors have told me that they avoided doing this and found that they had unresolved problems occur years later.

Earl Grollman, in *Suicide, Prevention, Intervention, Postvention*, writes: "Especially in a case of suicide the bereaved needs to pour out his heart. And what Sigmund Freud calls the 'ties of dissolution' are so vital and therapeutic, that is, the sharing with the survivor of both pleasant and unpleasant memories of the deceased."

The Process of Grief

Many of the stages you may encounter during the grief process are discussed in succeeding sections of this booklet. Reactions vary from person to person. There is no step-by-step formula to be followed. Many loose ends, ragged edges, flashbacks are encountered along the way. Sometimes the process is long, and often it is lonely; there is no timetable or particular sequence.

Suicide presents a much more complex mourning period than when a natural or accidental death occurs. It is an unfamiliar role.

Shock/Disbelief

Your first reaction to the suicide is one of shock, disbelief. You feel dazed, numb, like someone has anesthetized you and you are living out a dream/nightmare. It doesn't seem real. Fortunately, at this time, some of the pain is shut off.

Our older daughter described feeling shock: When first told about her brother's suicide, she felt as though a suit of armor was slowly slipping over her body. "It felt like a protective suit," she told me.

Dr. Arthur Freese, in *Help for Your Grief,* describes it like this: "Mercifully, nature covers the bereaved with a protective emotional blanket within minutes of the death news—there is a cold, empty numbness, a confused, dazed feeling of unreality that takes over."

Great Sadness

A week or perhaps several weeks after the suicide the numbness wears off and an overwhelming sense of sadness surfaces. I was totally unprepared for the sadness that hit me. The physical intensity of the pain surprised me. It's very personal—an individual aching that lingers and lingers. I've heard it described as a "toothache of the heart." Many survivors I've talked with have voiced this pain. One mother of a young teenage girl who chose an especially violent method of death said, "The pain I feel is so intimate! It's unbearable." Our younger daughter recently said to me, "Mom, I miss Sammy so much it hurts." I remember feeling like someone ripped open my chest and tore out my heart, leaving a big empty space.

Don't Hesitate to Get Professional Help

Seek professional help as soon as possible if you:

- Feel suicidal
- Feel like you are coming apart
- Feel out of control
- Have a history of severe emotional problems
- Have no one to talk with or to turn to
- Turn to alcohol, drugs, or other self-destructive behaviors like gambling, overeating, absence from work, poor relationships

Suicidal thoughts are not unusual for a survivor. You could have strong feelings to reunite with your loved one, or you might feel a need to escape your pain or that there is no reason to go on without your loved one. If you have suicidal thoughts, find a counselor. A professional can help you sort through your feelings.

Coming from a background in which you worked things out for yourself, I had no experience in seeking professional help. The professional my husband and I saw was extremely helpful. Dr. Edwin Shneidman, in his book *Death: Current Perspectives,* states: "Survivor-victims of such deaths [like suicide] are invaded by an unhealthy complex of disturbing emotions: shame, guilt, hatred, perplexity." I felt all these things and needed someone to help me.

Things Will Never Be the Same

At one of the counseling sessions, after my husband and I had expressed disbelief about our son's suicide, our counselor said, "This is your life. It will never again be the same as it was. You have lost your son and he will not return." It was a harsh truth that clarified a reality. Once spoken out loud, by an expert, whom we trusted, we could begin to accept the fact and face the reality that our lives would not be what they had been.

Ann Kaiser Stearns, in *Living Through Personal Crisis*, says: "Our losses change us and change the course of our lives. It's not that one can never again be happy following an experience of loss. The reality is simply that one can never again be the same."

Give Yourself Time

The mourning period is a time of convalescence when you face all those feelings that come to the surface. A dictionary definition of "convalescence" is: "Gradual return to health and strength after an illness. The period needed for this."

Note the words "gradual return . . . after an illness." Modern society doesn't think of the mourning period as an illness. Perhaps if it were thought of in that way, people would be more understanding and patient both to themselves and to others who are grieving. Unfortunately, we have a preconceived notion that after a few months, at the most a year, we'll be "better" and "back to normal." What is normal after a traumatic shock like suicide? You have never been through anything like this before. To get "better" takes time. It will take you a while to sort through the wreckage. Be kind to yourself. Give yourself permission to heal at your own pace.

Communicate with Your Family

Other members of your family will also be hurting. It's important to communicate with them and not to judge what they might be feeling or not feeling by your own experience. Be especially conscious of how children and adolescents are dealing with their grief. There will be many questions. We had family conferences right from the start, establishing open conversation, not hiding any of the facts from one another.

One question that came up for us was whether suicide was inherited. Experts all agree that suicide is not inherited or bequeathed from one to another genetically, but it can be imitated. One of our daughters had a great deal of concern that she, too, might be a victim of suicide when she reached the age her brother was when he completed suicide. I have heard other surviving brothers and sisters voice the same concern. Talking about these feelings can be life-preserving.

Tears

A song, a place, a familiar smell, almost anything can bring on a flood of tears. "It just hits me sometimes," a mother told me. Another survivor said, "I can't seem to stop crying. I do it everywhere, in the grocery store, car, at work, at home." Certain songs take me right back to a particular time and place, and the tears pour down my face.

Tears are nature's way of letting us express and release our pain. It is natural for some of us to weep a great deal. Some men think that it is inappropriate to cry; others might feel the need. My husband felt great relief after crying.

I felt like the tears washed away the cloud that surrounded my soul as it yearned for lost memories.

Guilt

Guilt is a major problem with suicide survivors. We seem to be obsessed with "if onlys." If only I had known! If only I had gotten home earlier! If only I hadn't said _____! If only _____!

Judy Tatelbaum writes, in *The Courage to Grieve:* "We preoccupy ourselves with 'if onlys,' ruminations in which we try to rewrite history to erase this disaster. Because we are so unprepared for loss in a sudden death, and because we usually have so much unfinished business with the deceased, sudden deaths seem to be the hardest with which to cope."

Most of us survivors have recurring guilt feelings over which we agonize. A good way to deal with the "if onlys" is to find an empathetic person who will listen to your feelings of self-blame and remind you of all the ways you are not to blame.

An empathetic listener can be a family member, pastor, social worker, neighbor, co-worker, doctor, friend, or support group who can listen to your feelings honestly and openly, who can give you reassurance and offer you hope when you feel none.

I had so many "if onlys." They went round and round in my head. Finally, our counselor asked why I didn't stop saying, "If only," and ask instead, "How are you going to live with this?"

Holidays, Birthdays, Etc.

Holidays, birthdays, anniversary dates, etc. are especially difficult times. You tend to compare the past good times with the sadness you now feel. The first year is filled with intense emotions, particularly stirred up on special occasions. Plan ahead for special days.

We dreaded facing the first anniversary date of our son's death. My husband and I planned ahead of time to spend the afternoon walking on the beach where our son had died, then to meet one of our daughters for dinner. More than likely you will feel down on this day too.

Anger

Do you feel angry? I did, and some of the survivors I've talked with have felt anger at various things:

- The medical profession (for not preventing the suicide)
- The deceased (for making you feel deserted, cheated, rejected)
- God (for not intervening)
- Teachers, friends, family members, classmates, etc.
- Yourself (for not preventing the suicide)
- The fact that this happened

One mother said to me, "I'm furious at the world. They couldn't even diagnose my daughter's problem. Why couldn't they have helped her?" Another said, "You bet I'm mad at my son. He cheated me out of my grandchildren. How dare he!" A surviving spouse said, "How could she have done something as vicious as shoot herself right in front of me? I did everything I could to help her." Another said, "My husband did this to get back at me. What a horrible thing to do to the children and me! We'll carry this with us forever."

John Hewitt, in *After Suicide*, says, "Survivors feel rage toward the deceased for publicly rejecting them. Suicide is a form of desertion, a way of saying 'I abandon you' for all to see. Anger is your natural response to such treatment."

If you find yourself feeling angry, find a way to express it. It helped me to express my feelings in a letter. Some professionals suggest keeping a journal, hitting a pillow, talking to an empty chair, etc. God wants to hear your anger too. Here is a way for you to tell God what you are feeling.

Are you listening, God?
I feel _____ (add your own feelings)
I feel pain
I feel angry
I feel joyless
I feel overwhelming sadness
I feel heartbroken
I want to pull the covers over my head and escape my pain.
Are you listening, God?

Searching/Pining

I remember driving home from work one night several months after our son's suicide, searching the streets for my son. My husband remembers the night he was watching a football game on TV several months after the death and is certain he saw our son in the crowd. We looked at each other and said, "I can't help looking for him. I want to find him."

Lily Pincus, in her book *Death and the Family*, talks about this: "Searching is the principal behavior pattern evoked by loss. Children and animals search for the absent object. The bereaved adult, even if he is aware of the irrational component in his behavior, keeps on searching for his dead, during unguarded moments, in hallucinations, and especially in dreams. . . . I wonder whether the impulse to search for the lost person ever completely disappears."

13

Why?

Why did this happen? Why would anyone choose to die? The motivations to suicide are usually complex. Each case is individual, and differs from one situation to another. Dr. Norman Farberow, a pioneering suicidologist and co-founder of the Los Angeles Suicide Prevention Center, writes, in *Youth Suicide:* "Many . . . factors influence the eventual act, . . . oftentimes these are so complex that each individual case must be explored in depth and evaluated in detail in order to obtain an understanding of the eventual culmination in a terminal self-destructive act." Various factors could be involved, such as physical or mental illness, abuse of alcohol or drugs, financial problems, social pressures, loss of a loved one, depression.

I've heard survivors offer a variety of reasons. A husband who lost his wife said, "My wife was depressed for a long time. Nothing I did seemed to help." A mother said of her young daughter's suicide, "Why couldn't she have waited? Didn't she know it would have gotten better?" A daughter who lost her mother said, "My mother always told us she didn't plan to live past the age of 70. None of us ever thought she actually meant it." A girlfriend said of her boyfriend, "He was always the one to reach out and help others. And he was so good at masking *his* problems. We didn't have any idea." A mother said of her young son's suicide, "I think he was saying, 'Open the door and let me out, I can't stand it here any longer!'"

Dr. Farberow says in *Essays of Self-Destruction,* "The suicidal [person] experiences overwhelming feelings of hopelessness and helplessness, feels incapable of working out any solutions . . . is unable to see other alternatives besides death."

I suspect our son had a number of reasons for completing suicide, ranging from depression, loss of self-esteem, loss of direction, loss of friends, and many more I will never know. Above all, I believe that he felt he had to end his unbearable pain and saw no other solution.

Stigma

Unfortunately, feelings of stigma, shame, embarrassment, a sense that our loved ones did something terribly wrong often goes along with the suicide death. John Hewitt, in *After Suicide,* describes it well: "[The] image of being branded probably describes pretty accurately how you feel." Some of these feelings are left over from years ago, when people felt strongly that suicide was considered to be a criminal, cowardly, or sinful act. The subject was not something that was openly discussed. With all the recent press coverage on suicide has come a better awareness of the problem, making it somewhat easier to talk about. In *Too Young to Die,* Francine Klagsbrun speaks to this issue: "Suicide in a family is not a shameful matter to be hidden away. It is a tragedy that destroys one life and disrupts many others."

My husband and I find it best to share honestly with people about our son's death, even if we occasionally sense an uneasiness.

Is God Punishing Us?

Have you wondered if God is punishing you for something you might or might not have done, causing you this terrible loss? Is God responsible for the suicide act? Was it the will of God?

I believe that when God created us, we were given

the power to reason and the freedom to make choices—even to live or die. Unfortunately, our loved ones made a decision we did not agree with. I suspect it was not God's choice either.

Shortly after his son's accidental death in a car, William Sloane Coffin, senior minister at Riverside Church in New York City, spoke about this in a sermon: "God doesn't go around this world with his finger on triggers, his fist around knives, his hands on steering wheels. God is dead set against all unnatural deaths. . . . My own consolation lies in knowing that it was not the will of God."

Believing that God was not responsible for the suicide helps us to understand that God is not punishing us.

Does God Forgive and Accept Our Loved One?

Have you pondered this question? It precipitated a great deal of searching for me. I know of only five accounts of suicide in the Old Testament: (1) Abimelech (Judges 9:50–54); (2) Samson (Judges 16:23–31); (3) Saul (1 Samuel 31:1–5; 2 Samuel 1:1–27); (4) Zimri (1 Kings 16:8–18); and (5) Ahithopel (2 Samuel 17:23). And some of those deaths could be classified as other than suicide in today's interpretation. In the New Testament, Judas is the only suicide: "Throwing down the pieces of silver in the temple, he departed; and he went and hanged himself [Matt. 27:5, RSV]." It is important to note that no place in the Bible are any of these persons recriminated against for their suicidal act.

Our faith teaches us much about God's sustaining love, mercy, and forgiveness. David speaks of God's love and forgiveness: "For thou, O Lord, art good and forgiving, abounding in steadfast love to all who call on thee [Ps. 86:5, RSV]." Throughout his ministry on earth, Jesus forgave people. His last words on earth were: "Father, forgive them; they do not know what they are doing [Luke 23:34, NEB]."

I agree with John Hewitt's words in *After Suicide:* "To make the last millisecond of a person's life so supremely important is to misunderstand both the worth of our lives and the forgiveness of God. Our lives aren't games of high-stakes poker, where one final hand can wipe you out. God judges our lives in their totality. If we accept the premise that God's nature is one of steadfast love and mercy, then we must say with Barth: 'If there is forgiveness of sins at all, . . . there is surely forgiveness for suicide.' " (Karl Barth, *Church Dogmatics*, Vol. III/4)

Where Is God?

Do you wonder where God is? Do you feel God has forsaken you, left you alone to suffer? Do you even question God's love?

Are these unspeakable, unnatural questions? When Job lost all his possessions, his health, his children, he "cursed the day of his birth. And Job said: 'Let the day perish wherein I was born [Job 3:1–3, RSV].' " Job's wife shouted, "Curse God and die [Job 2:9, RSV]." Even Jesus cried, from the cross, "My God, my God, why hast thou forsaken me?"

Roger Shinn's words, in *We Believe*, clarify God's presence: "When we ask [for] God's presence, whether in trial or rejoicing, he will be there. As a matter of fact, he will be there even if we do not invite him. But wanted or not, God is with us in trial and rejoicing."

Renewing Our Faith

Keeping the faith isn't easy when you've been stripped naked, your life shattered in smithereens. C.S. Lewis talks about facing this in *A Grief Observed*: "You never know how much you really believe anything until its truth or falsehood becomes a matter of life and death to you."

All my life I've had a strong, unshakable faith in God. My formative years were difficult. Although my father had a major depressive disorder—in a society that hid mental illness in the closet—my faith stood strong. Later, when my sister lost her young son to brain tumors, my faith also remained firm. But when Sammy died, my faith was shaken. There were so many questions and so little energy to work on them. Throughout this time, my husband and our minister encouraged me to continue to pray, attend church, and hold on. "It'll come," they both said. Reflecting on that time now, perhaps I was in a holding pattern, waiting to do what Kahlil Gibran expresses in his words about pain in *The Prophet*: "Accept the seasons of your heart, even as you have always accepted the seasons that pass over your fields." Easier said than done. Life had thrown me a devastating blow. Questioning God at that time, I seemed to get few answers—at least not the preconceived answers I wanted. Now some of my questions have found suitable answers; others have ceased to be important. I know God loves me and is with me.

My husband's quest has been a different kind of experience. His faith has not wavered throughout his grieving. It has remained firm and strong. He feels, and has felt, great comfort from God's continual presence.

Whatever your experience, I urge you to cast your burdens on God.

Adaptation/Reorganization

It takes a lot of personal strength to face and accept the death of a loved one by suicide and then to adapt and reorganize one's own life. Each of us must do it in his or her own time. Accepting the death doesn't mean that we have to like the situation or that we won't miss our loved ones.

Death gives us the opportunity to reevaluate everything in life. It teaches us to deal with important matters, to appreciate our families, friends, to look for new meaning in life. We now live life more in the present, realizing that time cannot be wasted.

As grieving persons, each of us needs to work through the process of grief. Each memory worked through. As you do this, you'll find your pain less all-consuming.

Surviving suicide is like traveling on a road that goes up and down various peaks and valleys. We must continue to move along that road, not to become trapped in a place where we might revolve our lives around the suicide. We are faced with a choice: to confront the pain, go through the process of mourning, and then to find a way to adapt and reorganize our lives; or, to linger in one of the valleys, dwelling on the suicide, not moving beyond the death itself.

C.S. Lewis, in *A Grief Observed*, discusses adaptation slowly occurring: "There are . . . two enormous gains. . . . Turned to God, my mind no longer meets that locked door; turned to [his deceased wife], it no longer meets that vacuum. . . . Both changes were not really observable. There was no sudden, striking . . . transition. When you first notice them they have already been going on for some time." Eventually, adaptation creeps into your life.

Responding

Responding means for you to grab hold of what has happened to you and to do something in spite of it. How you respond depends on you.

Harold Kushner, in *When Bad Things Happen to Good People,* writes: "We, by our responses, give suffering either a positive or a negative meaning. . . . If the death . . . of someone we love makes us bitter, . . . against all religion, and incapable of happiness, *we* turn the person who died into one of the 'devil's martyrs.' If . . . death in someone close to us brings us to explore the limits of our capacity for strength and love . . . *we* make the person into a witness for the affirmation of life rather than its rejection."

A young friend of our son had a serious drug problem for a number of years. After Sammy's death, he asked his father for help, went through a drug rehabilitation program, returned to college, and is now helping young people with their drug problems. A young battered mother, who lost her husband to suicide, was angry and bitter when left alone to bring up her two young children. She worked through her grief and went on to pursue her lifelong dream of becoming an artist. Our younger daughter was thrust into a difficult situation when her brother completed suicide. A junior in college, she was living in a dorm. Working through her grief wasn't easy in an environment that has no time for sadness of that magnitude. With a counselor and a caring support system, she was able to complete school and find herself a good job. My husband's and my response has been to work with survivors of suicide and to help educate others in a variety of ways about suicide. I know a wonderful woman, however, who hasn't been able to get beyond being angry and bitter.

She told me, "I'll never be happy again." She suffers greatly by her response.

A surviving mother of a son who completed suicide, Iris Bolton, having gone on to get her master's degree in suicidology, speaks, counsels, and works with survivors and various groups, including The Compassionate Friends (a national self-help organization for bereaved parents). She writes in her book *My Son . . . My Son . . .* : "You have taught me to revere life. I see that it is precious and can vanish in an instant. . . . What a treasury of lessons your sacrifice has uncovered."

Being willing to make a positive response can open up your world again. It can also bring you some peace.

Suggestions and Thoughts for Recovery

Here are some suggestions for you to think about during your mourning:

- Accept the loss.
- Face the pain.
- Don't be afraid to cry.
- Find an empathetic listener to share with.
- Be aware of your family's pain.
- Take good care of yourself, rest, eat well.
- Give yourself time to heal.
- Forgive yourself for any guilt you might feel.
- Remember, the choice was not yours.
- Don't panic if you have setbacks.
- Don't make rash or quick decisions.
- Don't be afraid to ask friends and family for help.
- Give yourself permission to be angry.
- Have a regular routine.

- Plan things to do—especially on special occasions and holidays.
- Remember, suicide is not inherited.
- Take life an hour or a day at a time.
- Keep in mind, you will survive.
- Talk to God.
- Find a support group in your area. Call the local suicide prevention center, ask your pastor about any grieving groups that might be available, call the local Compassionate Friends chapter, or ask your pastor to start a grief support group at your church.

Books That Might Be Helpful

In *Acquainted with Grief,* Adam Campbell Rose writes: "Death and sorrow are universal; there will be healing in the tears you shed over books." I find these books particularly helpful: Iris Bolton, *My Son . . . My Son . . .* (Atlanta: Bolton Press, 1983); Albert Cain, ed., *Survivors of Suicide* (Springfield, IL: Charles C. Thomas, 1972); Arthur Freese, *Help for Your Grief* (New York: Schocken Books, 1977); Earl A. Grollman, *Suicide Prevention, Intervention, Postvention* (Boston: Beacon Press, 1971) and *Talking About Death, A Dialogue Between Parent and Child* (Boston: Beacon Press, 1976); John H. Hewitt, *After Suicide* (Philadelphia: Westminster Press, 1980); Francine Klagsbrun, *Too Young to Die* (New York: Pocket Books, 1984); Harold Kushner, *When Bad Things Happen to Good People* (New York: Schocken Books, 1981); C.S. Lewis, *A Grief Observed* (New York: Bantam Books, 1976); Michael L. Peck, Norman L. Farberow, and Robert E. Litman, eds., *Youth Suicide* (New York: Springer Publishing Co., 1985); Lily Pincus, *Death and the Family: The Importance of Mourning* (New York: Vintage

Books, 1976); Ada Campbell Rose, *Acquainted with Grief* (Philadelphia: Westminster Press, 1972); Harriet Sarnoff Schiff, *The Bereaved Parent* (New York: Penguin Books, 1978); Edwin S. Shneidman, ed., *Death: Current Perspectives* (Palo Alto, CA: Mayfield Publishing Co., 1984); Kate W. Slagle, *Live with Loss* (Englewood Cliffs, NJ: Prentice-Hall, 1982); Ann Kaiser Stearns, *Living Through Personal Crisis* (Chicago: Thomas More Press, 1984); Judy Tatelbaum, *The Courage to Grieve* (New York: Harper & Row, 1980); Robert Veninga, *A Gift of Hope* (Toronto: Little, Brown & Co., 1985).

> Love is strong as death. . . .
> Many waters cannot quench love,
>   neither can floods drown it.
>   —Song of Solomon 8:6–7, RSV

> Love goes on forever.
>   —1 Corinthians 13:8, TB

But now he is dead; why should I fast? Can I bring him back again? I shall go to him, but he will not return to me.

>   —2 Samuel 12:23, RSV

Let Us Pray Together

Dear God:
In the past weeks, months, years,
our lives have changed dramatically.
Our loved one made a decision we wish she/he had
    not made,
leaving us heartbroken, with disbelief, guilt, anger,
confusion, so many "if onlys" and "whys?"
Help us to accept what has happened.
Help us to live with only partial answers.
Help us to find a way to cherish our memories.
Help us to adapt and reorganize our lives.
Help us to find a new focus.
Help us to respond in a positive way;
to go on with renewed faith in your everlasting love.
Amen.

Finally . . . the morning came,
after the mourning.